C000254576

CALLS
TO
WORSHIP

ROBERT I. VASHOLZ

'In the call to worship God calls us to give him praise, but the command is not onerous. It is an invitation to respond to God's revelation of himself and his grace. In offering this invitation God is both host and honoree, and God's people are both invited and compelled by his mercy to give him glory. God gives us the privilege of welcome into his presence that we might reciprocate with the gift of worship. Right perception of this gift exchange encourages the worship leader to speak the call to worship with the warmth of heart and openness of gesture that such an occasion of mutual blessing deserves.'

Bryan Chapell
Pastor, Grace Presbyterian Church, Peoria, Illinois

'...very simply a collection of "calls to worship" designed to encourage the congregation to turn to God and focus on him. There are different ideas for different events, from Easter to Baptism services, some uttered just by the pastor and those which require a response from the congregation.'

Christian Marketplace
Resourcing retailers and suppliers

CALLS
TO
WORSHIP

A Pocket Resource

ROBERT I. VASHOLZ

CHRISTIAN
FOCUS

Robert Vasholz was Chairman of the Old Testament Department at Covenant Theological Seminary, St Louis, Missouri for over twenty-five years. He completed his doctoral studies at the University of Stellenbosch in South Africa. His dissertation compared the Aramaic in Daniel and Ezra with 38 fragments of a Targum of Job uncovered among the Dead Sea Scrolls. He holds a degree from Covenant Theological Seminary and has enjoyed post-doctoral studies at Brandeis and Harvard. He has also written *The Old Testament Canon in the Old Testament Church* which has been reproduced in several languages. He is a native of Kansas City, Missouri. He and his wife, Julia, have one daughter and five grandchildren.

Copyright © Robert I. Vasholz

10 9 8 7 6 5 4 3 2 1

ISBN 978-1-84550-338-3

Published in 2008
Reprinted in 2020
by
Christian Focus Publications,
Geanies House, Fearn, Tain, Ross-shire,
IV20 1TW, Scotland, UK

www.christianfocus.com

Cover design by Daniel Van Straaten

Printed and bound by Gutenberg, Malta

PREFACE

The one who would benefit from this book will discover that this work is sectioned into three parts. The first section is designed to address specific events common to the Church such as Christmas, Easter, etc. The second section pertains to calls to worship that ask for anaudible response from God's people. The third part offers a number of calls to worship from the minister alone. It is my honest desire that this will serve as a proper and dignified way to enhance public corporate worship and to invite God's people to be attentive to the service that follows.

Robert I. Vasholz

**SEEK THE LORD
WHILE HE MAY BE FOUND
CALL UPON HIM
WHILE HE IS NEAR**

Make a joyful noise to the LORD, all the earth!
Serve the LORD with gladness!
Come into his presence with singing!
Know that the LORD, he is God!
It is he who made us, and we are his;
we are his people, and the sheep of his pasture.
Enter his gates with thanksgiving,
and his courts with praise!
Give thanks to him; bless his name!
For the LORD is good;
his steadfast love endures forever,
and his faithfulness to all generations.

(Ps. 100 ESV)

These joyful words of the Psalmist that call God's covenant people to worship exemplify the qualities of a call to worship that begins a worship service. In the common practice of Christian churches across many traditions, a call to worship typically is a few lines of Scripture (or a combination of Scripture texts) expressed by a minister or worship leader at the beginning of a church service. The call to worship exhorts God's people to turn from worldly distractions and to focus hearts, minds and actions on revering him. The beloved words of Psalm 100 well demonstrate the principles that for centuries have guided worship leaders in their expression and choice of words for the call to worship:

1) God calls us to worship. God's Word exhorts his people, 'Make a joyful noise to the LORD,' and 'Serve the LORD with gladness.' In writing these words under the inspiration of the Holy Spirit, the Psalmist is actually speaking for God as he calls the ancient people to worship. The example should remind us that a contemporary worship leader who uses the words of Scripture to call the congregation to worship still speaks in behalf of God. The host of the worship service is divine. We do not invite him to be present. He invites us to, 'Come into his presence' (v. 2). God calls us from all other preoccupations to join the people he has redeemed in recognition, praise and service of his omnipresent glory.

2) Because the call to worship is from God, we are reminded that he always initiates; we respond. This is a profound truth not only for our salvation, but also for our worship of the One who saves us. The call to worship is not simply a perfunctory greeting of human cordiality, but is at once a weighty responsibility and a joyful privilege. The worship leader issues God's invitation to join the heavenly throng that always praises him. The traditions of each church and occasion will help determine the appropriateness of gathering people from stray thoughts and conversations with informal words of welcome (e.g. 'Good morning. How good to have you here in God's house!'), but the privileges

and responsibilities of the call to worship that actually commences our focus on revering God are too good to displace with comments regarding the weather and yesterday's football game.

With a scriptural call to worship God invites us by his Word to join the worship of the ages and angels. God does not simply invite us to a party of friends, or a lecture on religion, or a concert of sacred music – he invites us into the presence of the King of the Universe before whom all creation will bow and for whom all heaven now sings. With the call to worship God's people are invited to participate in the wondrous praise that already and eternally enraptures the hosts of heaven. This awesome news and great privilege should be reflected with appropriate enthusiasm and joy by the worship leader in the call to worship. Such a call will typically lead directly into a corporate or choral hymn of praise as God's people respond to the blessings of worship into which they are called. A well-planned call to worship often reflects the theme of the service or the nature the occasion so that the remaining elements of service are a natural outflow of, and response to, the content of the call.

3) God calls us to respond to his revelation. By using the words of Scripture as a call to worship, the leader automatically urges God's people to respond to his disclosure of his own nature and purposes. This pattern established by the call to worship shapes the rest of the worship service. We do not approach God on our terms, but his. When he speaks, it is our obligation and privilege to respond appropriately in praise, prayer, repentance,

testimony, encouragement of others, and service to what he declares about himself. This corporate dialogue in which we as God's people respond to God's revelation is the sacred rhythm of covenant worship that begins with the call to worship.

God reveals himself in Psalm 100: 'Know that the LORD, he is God. It is he who made us…' (v. 3). This revelation of God as Lord and Creator immediately leads the Psalmist to exhortations for further exaltation: 'Enter his gates with thanksgiving and his courts with praise; give thanks to him; bless his name!' (v. 4). These words remind us that a call to worship has an imperative quality. We are not simply informing others of the attributes of God or creating a holy aura by the citation of a poignant Scripture passage. In the call to worship, the worship leader specifically calls God's people to respond to God's revelation.

Though it may seem obvious, it is often important to remind worship leaders that the text chosen for a call to worship is, in fact, a 'call.' In the call to worship the leader exhorts God's people to respond to the revelation of the divine nature and blessings. Thus, the text should call the people to shout, sing, praise, bow, bless or in some other way express their worship of God. If the text itself does not have this imperative aspect (and virtually all texts chosen as calls to worship in historic liturgies do possess such an imperative), then the worship leader should provide a word or phrase that instructs God's people how to respond to the text cited. An added phrase as simple as, 'In light of what God has told us about his love, let us worship him,' can turn a Scripture that has no 'call' quality into an appropriate call to worship.

4) God calls us to respond to his redemption. Because God invites our praise, we know our worship pleases him – somehow we have been made precious to him. The Psalmist does not merely remind us that God made us, but also '…we are his; we are his people, the sheep of his pasture' (v. 3). As we face our weakness, frailty and sin, it seems impossible that God would be pleased by us – or our praise. Yet, his invitation to worship is itself a revelation of his grace that makes us willing and able to respond to him. In fact, knowledge of God's redemptive qualities serves as the impetus for the climax of the Psalmist's call to worship. The Psalmist's adoration crescendos with these words: 'Enter his gates with thanksgiving and his courts with praise' (v. 4); and the reasons follow: 'For the LORD is good and his steadfast love endures forever; and his faithfulness to all generations' (v. 5).

The entire message of the Gospel is not usually verbalized in the call to worship, but its features inevitably glisten. By a scriptural call to worship we understand that God welcomes us to his presence and invites us to participate in his purposes. Though we are weak, he is welcoming; though our iniquities are great, he remains inviting. The call to worship necessarily and simultaneously commends God's worthiness and consoles us in our unworthiness. We can come to him; he wants us; and, he delights in our praise. All this reminds us that God has established our relationship with him by his grace and – far from releasing us from all holy obligations – that grace now compels our response of worship.

In the call to worship God calls us to give him praise, but the command is not onerous. It is an invitation to respond to God's revelation of himself and his grace. In offering this invitation God is both host and honoree, and God's people are both invited and compelled by his mercy to give him glory. God gives us the privilege of welcome into his presence that we might reciprocate with the gift of worship. Right perception of this gift exchange encourages the worship leader to speak the call to worship with the warmth of heart and openness of gesture that such an occasion of mutual blessing deserves.

Bryan Chapell, President,
Covenant Theological Seminary, St Louis, Missouri

I.

Calls to Worship

Special Occasions
including Church Calendar

Responsive:

Pastor:

Come, everyone who thirsts,
  Come without money and without price.
Incline your ear, and come to Me,
  hear that your soul may live.

Congregation:

For His flesh is true food and His blood is true drink.

  For on the last day of the great feast, Jesus stood up and cried out, 'If anyone thirsts, let him come to Me and drink.'

Scripture References

Isaiah 55:1, 3

John 6:55; 7:37

02 THE LORD'S SUPPER

Pastor Only:

Pastor:
> Great are the works of the Lord,
>   full of splendor and majesty;
> He remembers His covenant forever.
> He broke the bread and gave thanks;
> He said, 'This is my body which is for you.'

Scripture References

Psalm 111:2, 3, 5

1 Corinthians 11:22, 24

THE LORD'S SUPPER **03**

Pastor Only:

Pastor:
Christ, our Passover lamb, has been sacrificed for us.
Let us celebrate the festival, not with the old leaven, the leaven of malice and evil, but with the unleavened bread of sincerity and truth,

Scripture Reference

I Corinthians 5:7, 8

04 BAPTISM (Adult)

Responsive:

Pastor:
O Come, let us worship the God who has provided something better for us.

Congregation:
In Whom by His death we were baptized in Him that we might walk in the newness of life.

Scripture References

Hebrews 11:40;

Romans 6:4

Pastor Only:

Pastor:
Let us call upon the One who saved us, not because
of works done by us in righteousness, but according
to His own mercy, by the washing of regeneration
and renewal of the Holy Spirit,

Scripture Reference

Titus 3:5

06 BAPTISM (Children)

Responsive:

Pastor:
Let us welcome the One who said, 'Let the little children come to me and do not hinder them, for to such belongs the kingdom of heaven.'

Congregation:
For behold, children are a heritage from the Lord, the fruit of the womb a reward.

Scripture References

Matthew 19:14

Psalm 127:3

Pastor Only:

Pastor:
Come, O children and listen to me;
I will teach you the fear of the Lord.
Then the children shall see it and be glad:
their hearts shall be glad.

Scripture References

Psalm 34:11

Zechariah 10:7

Responsive:

Pastor:
He who said, 'I am the resurrection and the life.
Whoever believes in me, though he die, yet shall he
live,' calls us to attend Him.

Congregation:
Who also said, 'And everyone who lives and believe
in me shall never die.'

Scripture Reference

John 11:25-26

Responsive:

Pastor:

Blessed and holy is the one who shares in the first resurrection! Over such the second death has no power, but they will be priests of God and of Christ, and they will reign with him for a thousand years. All praise and glory to Him!

Congregation:

For with great power the apostles were giving their testimony to the resurrection of the Lord Jesus, and great grace was upon them all.

Scripture References

Revelation 20:6

Acts 4:33

10 EASTER

Pastor Only:

Pastor:
Grace to you and peace from Him Who is and Who was and Who is to come; even Jesus Christ the faithful witness, the firstborn of the dead, and the ruler of kings on earth.

To Him Who loves us and has freed us from our sins by His blood.

Scripture Reference

Revelation 1:4-5

Pastor Only:

Pastor:
O hear a call to worship, you who through Him are believers in God, who raised Christ from the dead and gave Him glory, so that your faith and hope are in God. For we know that He who raised the Lord Jesus will raise us also with Jesus and bring us with you into his presence.

Scripture Reference

I Peter 1:21

12 EASTER

Responsive:

Pastor:
O Come, let us worship for if we have died with Christ, we believe that we will also live with him.

Congregation:
For to this end Christ died and lived again, that He might be Lord both of the dead and of the living.

Scripture References

Romans 6:8; 14:9

Pastor Only:

Pastor:
If then you have been raised with Christ, let us seek the things that are above, where Christ is seated at the right hand of God.

Scripture Reference

Colossians 3:1

14 MARRIAGE

Responsive:

Pastor:
>Let us rejoice and exult and give God the glory,
>>for the marriage of the Lamb has come,
>>and His Bride has made herself ready.

Congregation:
>And the Spirit and the Bride say, 'Come.' And let the one who hears say, 'Come.' And let the one who is thirsty come; let the one who desires take the water of life without price.

Scripture References

Revelation 19:7; 22:17

Pastor Only:

Pastor:
Let us rejoice in the LORD;
   Let us exult in the God of our salvation,
for He has clothed us with the garments of salvation;
   He has covered us with the robe of righteousness,
as a bridegroom decks himself like a priest with a
   beautiful headdress,
   and as a bride adorns herself with her jewels.

Scripture Reference

Isaiah 61:10

16 MARRIAGE

Responsive:

Pastor:
Rejoice with those who rejoice.

Congregation:
For, as it is written, therefore a man shall leave his father and his mother and hold fast to his wife, and they shall become one flesh.

All:
Whom therefore God has joined together, let not man separate.

Scripture References

Romans 12:15

Genesis 2:24

Matthew 19:6

Pastor Only:

Pastor:
Rejoice before the Lord your God.
As a young man marries a young woman,
    so shall your sons marry you,
and as the bridegroom rejoices over the bride,
    so shall your God rejoice over you.

Scripture Reference

Isaiah 62:5

18 FUNERALS

Pastor Only:

Pastor:
Let us remember the One who said, 'I am the Alpha and the Omega,' says the Lord God, 'who is and who was and who is to come, the Almighty.'

'Fear not, I am the first and the last, and the living one. I died, and behold I am alive forevermore, and I have the keys of Death and Hades.'

Scripture References

Revelation 1:8, 17-18

Responsive :

Pastor:
If we have died with Him, we will also live with Him;
if we endure, we will also reign with Him;

Congregation:
For I am sure that neither death nor life, nor angels
nor rulers, nor things present nor things to come,
nor powers, nor height nor depth, nor anything else
in all creation, will be able to separate us from the
love of God in Christ Jesus our Lord.

Scripture References

2 Timothy 2:11-13

Romans 8:38, 39

20 FUNERALS

Pastor Only:

Pastor:
Let us rejoice in hope of the glory of God.

And hope does not put us to shame, because God's love has been poured into our hearts through the Holy Spirit who has been given to us.

For while we were still weak, at the right time Christ died for the ungodly.

Scripture References

Romans 5:2, 5, 6

Responsive:

Pastor:
Jesus invites us when He said, 'I am the resurrection and the life. Whoever believes in Me, though He die, yet shall He live, and everyone who lives and believes in Me shall never die.

Congregation:
Because I live, you also will live.

Scripture References

John 11:25-26; 14:19

---

22 FUNERALS

Pastor only:

Pastor:
> For I know that my Redeemer lives,
>> and at the last He will stand upon the earth.
>> and in my flesh I shall see God,
> Whom I shall see for myself,
>> and my eyes shall behold,
>> and not with others but with these same eyes.
> For He Who calls us is faithful to do it.

Scripture Reference

Job 19:25-27

Pastor Only:

Pastor:
Let us listen to the voice from heaven that says,
'Write this: Blessed are the dead who die in the
Lord from now on.' 'Blessed indeed,' says the Spirit,
'that they may rest from their labors, for their deeds
follow them!'

Scripture Reference

Revelation 14:13

---

24 ORDINATION

Pastor Only:

Pastor:

Before I formed you in the womb I knew you, and before you were born I consecrated you.

I chose you and appointed you that you should go and bear fruit and that your fruit should abide.

Scripture References

Jeremiah 1:5

John 15:16

Responsive:

Pastor:
You have loved righteousness and hated wickedness.
Therefore God, your God, has anointed you with
the oil of gladness beyond your companions;

Congregation:
To give them a beautiful headdress instead of ashes,
the garment of praise instead of a faint spirit;
that they may be called oaks of righteousness,
the planting of the Lord, that He may be glorified.

Scripture References

Psalm 45:7

Isaiah 61:3

---

26 DEDICATIONS

Responsive:

Pastor:
Know that the LORD has set apart the godly for Himself.

Congregation:
For the Lord said, You did not choose me, but I chose you and appointed you that you should go and bear fruit and that your fruit should abide.

Scripture References

Psalm 4:3

John 15:16

Pastor Only:

Pastor:

Commit your work to the LORD, and your plans will be established.

Let us render service with a good will as to the Lord and not to man, not by the way of eye-service, as people-pleasers, but as servants of Christ, doing the will of God from the heart.

Scripture References

Proverbs 16:3

Ephesians 6:6, 7

Responsive:

Pastor:
Hosanna! Blessed is He who comes in the name of the Lord!

Congregation:
May all kings fall down before Him,
    may all nations serve Him!

Scripture References

Mark 11:9

Psalm 72:11

Pastor Only:

Pastor:
Rejoice greatly, O daughter of Zion
    Shout aloud, O daughter of Jerusalem!
behold, your king is coming to you;
    righteous and having salvation is He,
    humble and mounted on a donkey,
    on a colt, the foal of a donkey.

Scripture Reference

Zechariah 9:9

30 PALM SUNDAY

Responsive:

Pastor:
Hosanna to the Son of David!
Blessed is He who comes in the name of the Lord!
Hosanna in the highest!
This is the prophet Jesus, from Nazareth of Galilee.

Congregation:
Therefore let us be grateful for receiving a kingdom
that cannot be shaken, and let us offer to God
acceptable worship, with reverence and awe.

Scripture References

Matthew 21:9, 11

Hebrews 12:28

Pastor Only:

Pastor:
Hosanna!
Blessed is He who comes in the name of the Lord!
Let us bow down toward your holy temple
and give thanks to your name
for your steadfast love and your faithfulness.

Scripture References

Mark 11:9

Psalm 138:2

32 REFORMATION DAY

Responsive:

Pastor:
> Let the peoples renew their strength;
> > let them approach, let us together draw near.

Congregation:
> Restore us to yourself, O LORD that we may be
> > restored!
> Renew our days as of old –

Scripture References

Isaiah 41:1

Lamentations 5:21

Pastor Only:

Pastor:
Return to Me, says the LORD of hosts, and I will return to you, says the LORD of hosts.

For in you our fathers trusted;
they trusted, and you delivered them.

Scripture References

Zechariah 1:3

Psalm 22:4

34 GOOD FRIDAY

Pastor Only:

Pastor:
He was despised and rejected by men;
a man of sorrows, and acquainted with grief;
and as One from whom men hide their faces
He was despised, and we esteemed Him not.
Surely He has borne our griefs.

Scripture Reference

Isaiah 53:3

Responsive:

Pastor:
He was wounded for our transgressions;
He was crushed for our iniquities;
upon Him was the chastisement that brought us peace,
and with His stripes we are healed.

Congregation:
All we like sheep have gone astray;
we have turned every one to his own way;
and the LORD has laid on him
the iniquity of us all.

Scripture References

Isaiah 53:5, 6

Pastor Only:

Pastor:
For Christ also suffered once for sins, the righteous for the unrighteous, that He might bring us to God, being put to death in the flesh but made alive in the spirit.

Scripture Reference

I Peter 3:18

Responsive:

Pastor:
>Hear my servant, whom I uphold,
>>my chosen, in whom my soul delights;
>
>He will not cry aloud or lift up his voice,
>>or make it heard in the street.
>
>A bruised reed He will not break,
>>and a faintly burning wick He will not quench.

Congregation:
>He will faithfully bring forth justice.
>>He will not grow faint or be discouraged
>
>till He has established justice in the earth;
>>and the coastlands wait for His law.

Scripture Reference

Isaiah 42:1-4

---

38 MAUNDY THURSDAY

Pastor Only:

Pastor:
> On the night of the Passaover, Jesus said to them, You will all fall away because of me this night. For it is written, I will strike the shepherd, and the sheep of the flock will be scattered. But after I am raised up, I will go before you to Galilee.

Scripture Reference

Matthew 26:31-32

Responsive:

Pastor:
And you, O Bethlehem, in the land of Judah,
are by no means least among the rulers of Judah;
for from you shall come a ruler Who will shepherd
my people Israel.

Congregation:
Proclaim it among the nations. Great indeed, is the
mystery of godliness:

Christ was manifested in the flesh,
vindicated by the Spirit,
seen by angels,
believed on in the world,
taken up in glory.

Scripture References

Matthew 2:6

I Timothy 3:16;

Pastor Only:

Pastor:
Have this mind among yourselves, which is yours in Christ Jesus,
     Being found in human form, he humbled himself by becoming obedient to the point of death, even death on a cross.

Scripture Reference

Philippians 2:5-8

Pastor Only:

Pastor:
Stand in awe before the Lord, for the Lord himself will give you a sign. Behold, the virgin shall conceive and bear a son, and shall call His name Immanuel.

Scripture Reference

Isaiah 7:14

Responsive:

Pastor:

Now the salvation and the power and the kingdom of our God and the authority of his Christ have come.

Congregation:

For to us a child is born,
to us a son is given;
and His name shall be called,
Wonderful Counselor, Mighty God,
Everlasting Father, Prince of Peace.

Scripture References

Revelation 12:10

Isaiah 9:6

II.

Responsive Calls to Worship

Pastor:

> Lift up your heads, O gates!
>> And be lifted up, O ancient doors,
>> that the King of Glory may come in.

Congregation:

> Who is this King of glory?

Pastor:

>> The LORD, strong and mighty,
>> the LORD, mighty in battle!
> Life up your heads, O gates!
>> that the King of glory may come in.

Congregation:

> Who is this King of glory?

All:

>> The LORD of hosts,
>> He is the King of glory.

Scripture Reference

Psalm 24:7-1

---

02 RESPONSIVE CALLS

Pastor:

Oh come, let us sing to the LORD;

> let us make a joyful noise to the rock of our salvation!

Let us come into His presence with thanksgiving;

> let us make a joyful noise to Him with songs of praise!

Congregation:

For the LORD is a great God,

> and a great King above all gods.

In His hand are the depths of the earth;

> the heights of the mountains are His also.

Scripture Reference

Psalm 95:1-2, 3-4a

Pastor:
> Oh come, let us worship and bow down;
>> let us kneel before the LORD, our Maker!

Congregation:
> For He is our God,
>> and we are the people of His pasture,
>> and the sheep of His hand.

Scripture Reference

Psalm 95:6-7

04 RESPONSIVE CALLS

Pastor:
> The LORD reigns;
>> let the peoples tremble!
> He sits enthroned upon the cherubim;
>> let the earth quake!
> Come, let them praise your great and awesome name!
>> For Holy is He!

Congregation:
> Exalt the LORD our God;
>> worship at His footstool!
>> For Holy is He!

Scripture References

Psalm 99:1, 3, 5

Pastor:
> Praise our God,
>> all you His servants,
> you who fear Him,
>> small and great.

Congregation:
> Hallelujah!
>> For the LORD our God the Almighty reigns.
> Let us rejoice and exult
>> and give Him the glory,
> for the marriage of the Lamb has come,
>> and His Bride has made herself ready.

Scripture Reference

Revelation 19:5-7

06 RESPONSIVE CALLS

Pastor:
> The LORD sits enthroned over the flood;
>> the LORD sits enthroned as king forever.

Congregation:
> Therefore let us ascribe to the LORD the glory due
>> His name;
> let us worship the LORD in the splendor of holiness.

Scripture References

Psalm 29:10, 2

Pastor:
> Oh, magnify the LORD with me,
>> and let us exalt His name together!
>
> Oh, taste and see that the LORD is good!

Congregation:
> Those who look to Him are radiant,
>> and their faces shall never be ashamed.

Scripture References

Psalm 34:3, 8, 5

---

08 RESPONSIVE CALLS

Pastor:
>Let the peoples praise you, O God;
>>let all the peoples praise you!
>
>Let the nations be glad and sing for joy,
>>for you judge the peoples with equity and guide
>>the nations upon earth. S

Congregation:
>Yes, let the peoples praise you, O God;
>>Let all the peoples praise you!

Scripture Reference

Psalm 67:3-5

Pastor:

> Let us sing to the LORD a new song;
>> Sing to the LORD, all the earth!
>
> Let us sing to the LORD, and bless His name;
>> Let us tell of His salvation from day to day.

Congregation:

> Let us declare His glory among the nations,
>> His marvelous works among all the peoples!

All:

> For great is the LORD, and greatly to be praised;
>> He is to be feared above all gods.

Scripture Reference

Psalm 96:1-4

10 RESPONSIVE CALLS

Pastor:
> Make a joyful noise to the LORD, all the earth;
>> break forth into joyous song and sing praises!

Congregation:
> The LORD has made known His salvation;
>> He has revealed His righteousness in the sight of
>> the nations.
> He remembers His steadfast love and faithfulness.

All:
> His right hand and his holy arm
>> have worked salvation for Him.
> For the LORD has made known His salvation.

Scripture Reference

Psalm 98

Pastor:

Give thanks to the LORD, for He is good,

Congregation:

for His steadfast love endures forever.

Pastor:

Give thanks to the God of gods,

Congregation:

for His steadfast love endures forever.

Pastor:

Give thanks to the LORD of LORDs,

Congregation:

for His steadfast love endures forever.

Scripture Reference

Psalm 136:1-3

---

12 RESPONSIVE CALLS

Pastor:
> Sing for joy, O heavens, and exult, O earth;
>> break forth, O mountains, into singing!

Congregation:
> for the LORD has comforted his people
>> and will have compassion on his afflicted.

Scripture Reference

Isaiah 49:13

Pastor:

O Lord, you are our God;
   we will exalt you; we will praise your name,
   for you have done wonderful things,
   plans formed of old, faithful and sure.

Congregation:

Strong peoples will glorify you;
   cities of ruthless nations will fear you.
For you have been a stronghold to the poor,
   a stronghold to the needy in his distress,
a shelter from the storm
   and a shade from the heat.

Scripture Reference

Isaiah 25:1, 3. 4

14 RESPONSIVE CALLS

Pastor:
> We offer thanks to you, LORD God Almighty,
>> Who is and Who was,
> for you have taken your great power
>> and begun to reign.

Congregation:
> All your works shall give thanks to you, O LORD,
>> and all your saints shall bless you!

Scripture References

Revelation 11:17

Psalm 145:10

Pastor:
> Come all the ends of the earth.
>> Remember and turn to the LORD,
> and let all the families of the nations
>> worship before you.

All:
> For this we come, O LORD, from among the nations,
>> to sing to your name.
> That all the ends of the earth remember and turn
> to the LORD and that all the families of the nations
> worship before you.

Scripture References

Psalm 22:27; 18:49

---

16 RESPONSIVE CALLS

Pastor:
Serve the Lord with fear,
    rejoice and come before Him with trembling.

Congregation:
Kiss the Son, lest he be angry,
    and you perish in the way,
for his wrath is quickly kindled.
    Blessed are all who take refuge in him.

Scripture Reference

Psalm 2:11, 12

Pastor:

Let us bless the L ORD
from this time forth and forevermore.
Praise the L ORD!

Congregation:

Come, let us go up to the mountain of the L ORD,
to the house of the God of Jacob,
that He may teach us His ways
and that we may walk in His paths.

Scripture References

Psalm 115:18

Isaiah 2:3

18 RESPONSIVE CALLS

Pastor:
> Come, let us walk
>> in the light of the Lord.

Congregation:
> Let us join ourselves to the LORD
>> in an everlasting covenant
>> that will never be forgotten.

Scripture References

Isaiah 2:5

Jeremiah 50:5

Pastor:

Let us go to His dwelling place;
let us worship at His footstool!

Congregation:

Let us draw near with a true heart in full assurance of faith, with our hearts sprinkled clean from an evil conscience and our bodies washed with pure water.

Scripture References

Psalm 132:7

Hebrews 10:22

20 RESPONSIVE CALLS

Pastor:
> Call a solemn assembly.
> Gather the elders
>> and all the inhabitants of the land
>> to the house of the LORD your God.

Congregation:
> For the LORD your God is merciful God. He will not
> leave you or destroy you or forget the covenant
> with your fathers that He swore to them.

Scripture References

Joel 1:14

Deuteronomy 4:31

Pastor:

    Praise the LORD!

        Oh give thanks to the LORD, for He is good,
        for His steadfast love endures forever!

Congregation:

    Praise the Lord!

        We will give thanks to the Lord with our whole
        heart, in the company of the upright, in the
        congregation.

Scripture References

Psalm 106:1; 111:1

22 RESPONSIVE CALLS

Pastor:
> Let us offer sacrifices of thanksgiving,
>> and tell of His deeds in songs of joy!

Congregation:
> Let us break forth together into singing,
>> for the Lord has comforted His people;
>> He has redeemed Jerusalem.

Scripture References

Psalm 107:22

Isaiah 52:9

Pastor:
Let us shout for joy over your salvation.

Congregation:
Shout, and sing for joy, O inhabitant of Zion,
for great in your midst is the Holy One of Israel.

Scripture References

Psalm 20:5

Isaiah 12:6

24 RESPONSIVE CALLS

Pastor:
> Let the righteous one rejoice in the LORD
> > and take refuge in him!
> > Let all the upright in heart exult!

Congregation:
> Let us greatly rejoice in the LORD;
> > for He has clothed us with the garments of salvation;
> > He has covered us with the robe of righteousness.

Scripture References

Psalm 64:10

Isaiah 61:10

Pastor:
Be exalted, O Lord, in your strength!
That we may sing and praise your power.

Congregation:
Sing praises to the Lord, O you His saints,
and give thanks to His holy name.

Scripture References

Psalm 21:13

Psalm 30:4

---

26 RESPONSIVE CALLS

Pastor:
Come, bless the LORD, all you servants of the LORD,
who stand in the house of the LORD!

Congregation:
Be exalted, O LORD, in your strength!
We will sing and praise your power.

Scripture Reference

Psalm 134:1

Pastor:
> The rich and the poor meet together;
>> the LORD is the maker of them all.

Congregation:
> We will be glad and exult in you;
>> We will sing praise to your name, O Most High.

Scripture Reference

Proverbs 22:2

Psalm 9:2

28 RESPONSIVE CALLS

Pastor:
Come now, let us reason together, says the LORD:
Though your sins are like scarlet,
    they shall be as white as snow;
though they are red like crimson,
    they shall become like wool.

Congregation:
Blessed is the one whose transgression is forgiven,
    whose sin is covered.

Scripture References

Isaiah 1:18

Psalm 32:1

Pastor:

Let the redeemed of the LORD say so,
whom He has redeemed from trouble.

Congregation:

Sing, O heavens, for the LORD has done it;
shout, O depths of the earth;
break forth into singing, O mountains,
O forest, and every tree in it!
For the LORD has redeemed His people.

Scripture References

Psalm 107:2

Isaiah 44:23

Pastor:
> Blessed be the LORD God of Israel,
>> for He has visited and redeemed his people.

Congregation:
> Declare this with a shout of joy,
>> proclaim it,
> send it out to the end of the earth;
>> say, 'The LORD has redeemed His servants.'

Scripture References

Luke 1:68

Isaiah 48:20

Pastor:
> Listen to me, all the remnant
>> who have been borne by me from before your
>> birth, carried from the womb.

Congregation:
> For we have received blessing from the Lord
>> and righteousness from the God of our salvation.

Scripture References

Isaiah 46:3

Psalm 24:5

Pastor:
May the LORD give strength to his people!
May the LORD bless his people with peace!

Congregation:
Then we will bless you as long as we live;
in your name we lift up our voices.

Scripture References

Psalm 29:11

Psalm 63:4

Pastor:

May God be gracious to us and bless us
and make His face to shine upon us.

Congregation:

Let us bless our God;
let the sound of His praise be heard from our lips.

Scripture Reference

Psalm 67:1

---

34 RESPONSIVE CALLS

Pastor:
> Seek the LORD and His strength;
>> seek His presence continually!

Congregation:
> Let us seek the LORD while He may be found;
>> Let us call upon Him while He is near.

Scripture References

Psalm 105:4

Isaiah 55:6

Pastor:
Thus says the LORD,
Seek me and live.

Congregation:
For here we have no lasting city, but we seek the city
that is to come.

Scripture Reference

Amos 5:4

Pastor:

Let us now worship God, who is a Spirit, in spirit and in truth.

Congregation:

For such the Father seeks to worship him.

Scripture Reference

John 4:23-24

III.

Calls to worship
by the Pastor only

Pastor:

Come and see what God has done:

He is awesome in His deeds toward the children of man.

Shout for joy to God, all the earth;

sing the glory of His name;

give to Him glorious praise!

Scripture Reference

Psalm 66:5, 1, 2

Pastor:
Make a joyful noise to the LORD, all the earth!
   Serve the LORD with gladness!
   Come into His presence with singing!
Know that the LORD, He is God!
   It is He who made us, and we are His;
   we are His people, and the sheep of His pasture.

Scripture Reference

Psalm 100:1-3

Pastor:

Let us lift our voices and exclaim that

'Worthy is the Lamb, who was slain, to receive power and wealth and wisdom and might and honor and glory and blessing.'

Scripture Reference

Revelation 5:12

Pastor:
> Praise the LORD!
> Praise, O servants of the LORD,
>> praise the name of the LORD!
> Let us bless the name of the LORD
>> from this time forth and forevermore!
> From the rising of the sun to its setting,
>> let the name of the LORD be praised!

Scripture Reference

Psalm 113:1-3

Pastor:

Come, let us bless the God and Father of our LORD Jesus Christ! Who, according to His great mercy has caused us to be born again to a living hope through the resurrection of Jesus Christ, to an inheritance imperishable, undefiled, and unfading, kept in heaven for us.

Scripture Reference

1 Peter 1:3

Pastor:

Join together. Let us sanctify the name of God forever and ever, to Whom belongs wisdom and might; Who changes times and seasons; removes and sets up kings; gives wisdom to the wise and knowledge to those who have understanding. To You, O God, we offer thanks and praise.

Scripture Reference

Daniel 2:20-22

Pastor:

Clap your hands, all peoples!
  Shout to God with loud songs of joy!
For the LORD, the Most High, is to be feared,
  a great king over all the earth.
Sing praises to God, sing praises!
Sing praises to our King, sing praises!

Scripture Reference

Psalm 47:1, 2, 6

Pastor:

> O LORD God of hosts, hear our prayer;
>> give ear, O God of Jacob!
> Blessed are those whose strength is in You;
>> who dwell in your house, ever singing your praise!
> Who go from strength to strength,
>> till each one appears before God in Zion.
> O LORD God of hosts, hear our prayer.

Scripture Reference

Psalm 84:1, 5, 7

Pastor:
It is good to give thanks to the LORD,
    to sing praises to your name, O Most High;
to declare your steadfast love in the morning,
    and your faithfulness by night;
For you, O LORD, have made me glad by your work;
    at the works of your hands let us sing for joy.

Scripture Reference

Psalm 92:1, 2, 4

---

10 FROM THE PASTOR

Pastor:

For you, O LORD, do we wait;
O my God, be not far from us!
Make haste to help us,
    O LORD, of our salvation!

Scripture Reference

Psalm 38:15, 21, 22

Pastor:
Bless the LORD, O you his angels,
    you mighty ones who do his word,
    obeying the voice of his word!
Bless the LORD, all his hosts,
    His ministers, who do his will!
Bless the LORD, all his works,
    in all places of His dominion.
Bless the LORD, O my soul!

Scripture Reference

Psalm 103:20-22

Pastor:

> To the church of God; to those sanctified in Christ Jesus, called to be saints together with all those who in every place call upon the name of our Lord Jesus Christ,
>
> Praise the Lord!
> For it is good to sing praises to our God;
>> for a song of praise is fitting.

Scripture References

I Corinthians 1:2

Psalm 147:1

Pastor:

Let the righteous one rejoice in the LORD
and take refuge in him!
Let all the upright in heart exult!

Scripture Reference

Psalm 64:10

Pastor:
Sing to God, sing praises to His name;
  lift up a song to Him who rides through the deserts;
His name is the LORD;
  exult before Him!

Scripture Reference

Psalm 68:4

Pastor:
Praise the LORD, all nations!
Extol him, all peoples!
For great is his steadfast love toward us,
and the faithfulness of the LORD endures forever.
Come, Let us praise the LORD!

Scripture Reference

Psalm 117

16 FROM THE PASTOR

Pastor:
This is the day that the Lord has made;
let us rejoice and be glad in it.

Scripture Reference

Psalm 118:24

Pastor:
Be glad in the Lord, and rejoice, O righteous,
and shout for joy, all you upright in heart!
We will wait for your name, for it is good,
in the presence of the godly.

Scripture Reference

Psalm 32:11; 52:9

Pastor:

Give thanks to our God always because of the grace of God that was given you in Christ.

Give thanks in all circumstances; for this is the will of God in Christ Jesus for you.

Scripture References

I Corinthians 1:4;

I Thessalonians 5:18

Pastor:

Open the gates of righteousness,
that we may enter through them
and give thanks to the LORD.

Let us go at once to entreat the favor of the LORD
and to seek the LORD of hosts.

Scripture References

Psalm 118:19

Zechariah 8:21

Pastor:
Seek the Lord while He may be found;
call upon him while He is near.
Then you shall call, and the Lord will answer;
you shall cry, and He will say, 'Here I am.'

Scripture References

Isaiah 55:6; 58:9

Pastor:

Hear this, all peoples!

Give ear, all inhabitants of the world.

Blessed are those who are invited to the marriage supper of the Lamb.

Scripture References

Psalm 49:1

Revelation 19:9

Pastor:
> The Mighty One, God the LORD,
>> speaks and summons the earth
>> from the rising of the sun to its setting.
> Gather to me my faithful ones,
>> who made a covenant with me by sacrifice!

Scripture Reference

Psalm 50:1, 5

Pastor:
Behold, this is our God;
we have waited for Him, that he might save us.
This is the LORD; we have waited for Him;
let us be glad and rejoice in His salvation.'

Scripture Reference

Isaiah 25:9

Pastor:
  Let us lift up our hearts and hands
      to God in heaven
      and return to the LORD.

Scripture Reference

Lamentations 3:40, 41

Pastor:
Let us know;
let us press on to know the Lord;
His going out is sure as the dawn;
He will come to us as the showers,
as the spring rains that water the earth.

Scripture Reference

Hosea 6:3

Pastor:

Come, Let us through Him continually offer up a sacrifice of praise to God, that is, the fruit of lips that acknowledge His name.

Scripture Reference

Hebrew 13:15

Pastor:

Let us praise the name of God together with a song.
Let us magnify Him together with thanksgiving.
With our mouths let us give great thanks to the LORD.

Scripture Reference

Psalm 69:30; 109:30

Pastor:
> Those who seek him shall praise the Lᴏʀᴅ!
> May your hearts live forever!

Scripture Reference

Psalm 22:26

Pastor:

Let the peoples gather together,
and kingdoms, to worship the LORD. For the LORD
will not forsake His saints.
They are preserved forever.

Scripture References

Psalm 102:22; 37:28

Pastor:

Exalt the LORD our God,
for the LORD our God is holy!

For the LORD God bestows favor and honor.
No good thing does He withhold
from those who walk uprightly.

Scripture References

Psalm 99:9; 84:11

Pastor:

Praise the LORD, for the LORD is good;
sing to His name, for it is pleasant!

Scripture Reference

Psalm 135:3

Pastor:
> We give thanks to you, O LORD my God, with our whole heart,
> we will glorify your name forever.

Scripture Reference

Psalm 86:12

Pastor:

Let every creature in heaven and on earth and under the earth and in the sea, and all that is in them, say,

'To Him who sits on the throne and to the Lamb be blessing and honor and glory and might forever and ever!'

Scripture Reference

Revelation 5:13

Pastor:
> Let us lift up the cup of salvation
>> and call on the name of the LORD.
> Let us offer the sacrifice of thanksgiving
>> and call on the name of the LORD.

Scripture Reference

Psalm 116:13, 17

Pastor:

> The LORD is near to all who call on Him,
>> to all who call on Him in truth.
>
> Therefore let us give thanks to the LORD,
>> call upon His name,
>> make known His deeds among the peoples,
>> proclaim that His name is exalted.

Scripture References

Psalm 145:18

Isaiah 12:4

Pastor:
> Shout for joy in the LORD, O you righteous!
>> Praise befits the upright.
>
> Let those who delight in His righteousness
>> shout for joy and be glad and say evermore,
> 'Great is the LORD, who delights in the welfare of
>> His servants!'

Scripture References

Psalm 33:1; 35:27

Pastor:

> My lips will shout for joy,
>> when I sing praises to you;
>> my soul also, which you have redeemed.
>
> Let us sing aloud to God our strength;
>> Let us shout for joy to the God of Jacob!

Scripture References

Psalm 71:23; 81:1

Pastor:
>Sing aloud, O daughter of Zion;
>>Shout, O Israel!
>Rejoice and exult with all your heart.
>For the LORD waits to be gracious to you.

Scripture References

Zephaniah 3:14

Isaiah 30:18

Pastor:

Let us now with meekness and boldness enter into the most holy place by the blood of Jesus, which He has opened for us.

Scripture Reference

Hebrews 10:19, 20

Robert Vasholz

BENEDICTIONS
A POCKET RESOURCE

ISBN 978-1-84550-230-0

BENEDICTIONS

A Pocket Resource

Robert Vasholz

Benedictions, invocations to depart with God's blessings, are a feature of the church - every liturgical structure ends with them. They were a feature of the synagogue in Christ's time – indeed Christ himself uses them when he dismisses his disciples on a new task. The word benediction derives from two Latin words that mean "to speak well of".

Benedictions are pronounced by ministers at the close of worship services as an expression of hope and encouragement to God's people to face whatever their future might hold. This makes them a Biblical norm for the end of worship – something we should consider doing each time we leave God's presence and go out into the world. If you are involved with leading worship in the church or in the home your next question will be 'Where do I go to find them?' Fortunately Robert Vasholz has done the legwork for you. He has collected in this one book the benedictions found in scripture along with some additional scripture enriched blessings for use during worship.

Use them to help Christians have a greater effect on the world.

'Robert Vasholz has collected many of the Bible's benedictions and constructed other scripture-enriched blessings for the use of ministers who lead worship. Indeed all Christians will be "blessed" by reading and praying these wonderful words from God.'

David Calhoun,
Professor of Church History, Covenant Theological Seminary,
St Louis, Missouri

David Short with David Searle

PASTORAL VISITATION
A POCKET MANUAL

FOR VISITING SOMEONE AT HOME OR IN HOSPITAL

ISBN 978-1-84550-0160

Pastoral Visitation

A Pocket Manual

David Short with David Searle

Visiting the sick, lonely or downcast is a duty we all have as Christians. It is not to be left to ministers or elders but is a responsibility for all those who seek to follow Christ's perfect example. The problem often arises when we actually make the visit. Discussing the weather or the hospital food is all very well but for our visit to have maximum value we need to try and help the person spiritually. Reading our favourite Bible passage might suffice once but it cannot be apt to every situation and what happens when you visit for a second time?

This is where this book helps. Providing Scripture readings, a prayer and even a suggested hymn for a wide range of possible visits it is a wonderfully useful tool. Written by authors with long pastoral experience it will prove a real help to all those who seek to turn the routine visit into a time of real spiritual growth.

A Consultant Cardiologist at Aberdeen Royal Infirmary for some 25 years, David Short was appointed Physician to Her Majesty the Queen and then Emeritus Professor of Clinical Medicine at the University of Aberdeen. In addition to his medical career he was both a preacher of God's Word and a pastor, particularly to the sick, bereaved and discouraged. He died in May 2005.

Until his retirement in 2005 David Searle was Director of Rutherford House, a theological research and study centre in Edinburgh. Prior to that he pastored a number of church in Scotland and Northern Ireland.

Leviticus

A MENTOR COMMENTARY

Robert I. Vasholz

ISBN 978-1-84550-044-3

LEVITICUS

A Mentor Commentary

Robert Vasholz

'Dr Vasholz claims that Leviticus, far from being a book to avoid or skip over, is of basic importance to the Bible and to our understanding of what it teaches. His commentary proves the claim to the hilt. It is a high treat to enter into huge scholarship wedded to patient, detailed explanation and exposition of the sacred text. Here is Leviticus brought out of obscurity into the light, off the sidelines into the mainstream. The patience of his scholarship calls for patience in our reading, and rewards it.'

Alec Motyer

'Vasholz's commentary on Leviticus provides another helpful resource for students of the Scriptures. His work on this often-neglected biblical book will take its place next to a comparatively small group of commentaries that combine an evangelical focus, a high view of Scripture, careful attention to the text, and an avoidance of overemphasis on symbolism and typology. Throughout the volume, he interacts with other commentaries on Leviticus as well as various monographs, writes clearly in an expositional fashion, and provides helpful explanations of a book whose meaning and importance eludes many of its readers.'

Michael A Grisanti,
Professor of Old Testament, The Master's Seminary, Sun Valley,
California

Christian Focus Publications

Our mission statement –

STAYING FAITHFUL

In dependence upon God we seek to impact the world through literature faithful to His infallible Word, the Bible. Our aim is to ensure that the Lord Jesus Christ is presented as the only hope to obtain forgiveness of sin, live a useful life and look forward to heaven with Him.

Books in our adult range are published in four imprints:

CHRISTIAN
FOCUS

Popular works including biographies, commentaries, basic doctrine and Christian living.

CHRISTIAN
HERITAGE

Books representing some of the best material from the rich heritage of the church.

MENTOR

Books written at a level suitable for Bible College and seminary students, pastors, and other serious readers. The imprint includes commentaries, doctrinal studies, examination of current issues and church history.

CF4•K

Children's books for quality Bible teaching and for all age groups: Sunday school curriculum, puzzle and activity books; personal and family devotional titles, biographies and inspirational stories – because you are never too young to know Jesus!

Christian Focus Publications Ltd,
Geanies House, Fearn, Ross-shire,
IV20 1TW, Scotland, United Kingdom.
www.christianfocus.com